Happy
Easter to
Mark!

Po Po
Yeh Yeh
4/2000

2 4 6 8 10 9 7 5 3

Published in 1998 by Sterling Publishing Company, Inc.
387 Park Avenue South, New York, NY 10016

Compilation of excerpts from
World's Punniest Joke Book by Mike Benny,
World's Wildest Animal Jokes by Francis Murray,
Shake, Riddle & Roll, and *Riddlemania* by Lori Miller Fox,
and *Biggest Riddle Book in the World,* and *Spooky Riddles*
by Joseph Rosenbloom

Manufactured in the United States of America

Sterling ISBN 0-8069-4805-1

GIANT BOOK OF RIDDLES

BY
MIKE BENNY   FRANCIS MURRAY
LORI MILLER FOX
&
JOSEPH ROSENBLOOM

ILLUSTRATIONS BY
SANFORD HOFFMAN

Sterling Publishing Company, Inc.
New York

Contents

1

Say It Ain't So!

What did the jellybean say to the Snickers Bar?
"Smile, you're on candied camera."

What did the wise old canary say to the parrot?
"Talk is cheap-cheap."

What did one canned mushroom say to the other canned mushroom?
"There's not mushroom (much room) in here."

What did the sock say to the needle?
   "I'll be darned."

What did the scarf say to the hat?
   "You go on ahead, I'll hang around."

What did the nylons say to the garter belt?
   "Make it snappy. I've got a run."

What did the shoe say to the shoelace?
   "Forget me knot."

What did the baked potato say to the cook?
   "Foiled again!"

What did the police say when a famous drawing was stolen?
   "Details are sketchy."

What did the coffee say to the police?
    "I've been mugged."

What did the comedian say to the cattle rancher?
    "Herd any good ones lately?"

What did the farmer say when he saw three holes in the ground?
    "Well, well, well!"

What did the farmer say when he lost the butter?
    "It'll churn up."

What do you say to curtains?
    "Pull yourself together."

What do you say to a guy who took 20 years to write a book about clock repair?
    "It's about time."

What do you say to your piano teacher?
    "Get off my Bach."

What do you say to a person who wakes up with a black eye?
    "Rise and shine-r."

What do hens say every morning?
    "Snap, cackle, pop."

What do you say to a closet?
 "Clothes the door."

What did the priest say to the salesman?
 "Nun for me."

What did the minister say to the stranger?
 "Your faith looks familiar."

What do you say to a stubborn tailor?
 "Suit yourself."

What do you say to a nudist?
 "Clad to see you."

What do you say to a stubborn chimney sweep?
 "Soot yourself."

What do you say to a stubborn lawyer?
 "Sue-it yourself."

What do you say to a baby in designer clothes?
 "Gucci Gucci goo."

What do you say to a king who falls off his chair?
"Throne for a loop?"

What do you say to a guy driving a car with no engine?
"How's it going?"

What do you say to an annoying car mechanic?
"Give me a brake (break)."

What do you say to introduce a hamburger?
"Meat Patty."

What do you say to a boomerang on its birthday?
"Many happy returns."

2
Why Oh Why?

Why did the undertaker write a book?
He had a good plot.

Why was the undertaker so nervous putting on a play?
He didn't have time to re-hearse.

Why did the cottage go on a diet?
It wanted to be a lighthouse.

Why did the sailor jump rope?
  He hoped he'd become the skipper.

Why didn't the skeleton cross the road?
  It didn't have the guts.

Why did the ghost apologize?
  It spook out of turn.

Why did the dynamite always get what it wanted?
  No one could re-fuse it.

Why didn't the kitchen window like the livingroom window?
  Because it was such a big pain (pane).

Why was the dumbbell late?
  It got held up at the gym.

Why did the plumber start dancing?
  He knew a little tap.

Why was the plumber so tired?
  He felt drained.

Why didn't the elephant buy a Porsche?
It had no trunk space.

Why did the cow jump over the moon?
To make a milky way.

Why did the garbage collector go on a diet?
He was worried about his waste-line (waistline).

Why did the pinky go to jail?
He was fingered by the police.

Why does it take so long to make a politician-snowman?
You have to hollow out the head first.

Why do gamblers love Ireland?
   They keep Dublin their odds.

Why didn't the weatherman ever get tired?
   He always got a second wind.

Why didn't the weatherman call for more wind?
   He thought it was dis-gusting.

Why did the farmer take two aspirins before going to the cornfield?
   In case he got an ear-acre (ache).

How did the carpenter break all his teeth?
   From chewing his nails.

Why did the silly kid take a whip and chair to the Improv?
   He heard the jokes were wild.

Why do nuns watch soap operas?
   They get into the habit.

3
Did You Hear...?

Did you hear about the street vendor who sold pudding?
It was custard's (Custer's) last stand.

Did you hear about the helpful policeman?
He was on the ad-vice squad.

Did you hear about the model at the debate?
She posed a good question.

Did you hear the joke about the mountain climber?
He hasn't made it up yet.

Did you hear about the sword swallower who worked for nothing?

He was a free-lancer.

Did you hear about the musician who was upset?

He couldn't compose himself.

Did you hear about the absent-minded musician?

He finally left himself notes.

Did you hear about the artist with a poor memory?

He kept drawing a blank.

Did you hear about the street-corner artist?

He had no trouble drawing a large crowd.

Did you hear about the kid who was twenty minutes early for school?

He was in a class by himself.

Did you hear about the kid who didn't like something about school?

It was the principal (principle) of the thing.

Did you hear about the actors in the paper-towel commercial?

There were four rolls (roles).

Did you hear about the cattle rancher at the poker game?

He kept raising the steaks (stakes).

Weather or Not

Did you hear about the weatherman who went back to college?

He got several degrees.

Did you hear about the weatherman who won the race?

He said it was a breeze.

Did you hear about the world's best weatherman?

He's the raining (reigning) champion.

Did you hear about the cowboy in the leaves?

He was accused of rustling.

Did you hear about the couple married in a bathtub?

They wanted a double ring ceremony.

Did you hear about the nudist runner?

She could do the hundred yard dash in nothing.

Did you hear about the glue truck that overturned?

Police were asking motorists to stick to their own lanes.

Did you hear about the soldier who wanted to be a pastry chef?

He was a desserter (deserter).

Did you hear about the deck chair factories that lost money?

They folded.

Did you hear about the class bully who was thrown out of the library?

He was hitting the books too hard.

Did you hear about the accident at the soup factory?
Two workers got canned.

Did you hear about the job at the coffee-maker factory?
It doesn't pay much, but there are lots of perks.

Did you hear about the nearsighted logger?
What he couldn't see the chain saw.

Did you hear about the 30-year-old butcher?
He was in his prime.

Did you hear about the needle that told jokes?
It could keep you in stiches.

Did you hear the story about the bed?
It was just made up.

Balmy in the Army

Did you hear about the doctor who joined the army?

He was a general practitioner.

Did you hear about the investigator who joined the army?

He was a private eye.

Did you hear about the umpire who joined the army?

He moved from base to base.

Did you hear about the absent-minded train conductor?
He lost track of things.

Did you hear about the school bus that had to repeat a grade?
Its brakes failed.

Did you hear about the boarding house that blew up?
Roomers (rumors) were flying.

Did you hear about the fish that got a face-lift?
He went to a plastic sturgeon (surgeon).

Did you hear about the healthy dressmaker?
She seamed (seemed) well.

Did you hear about the superhero who worked at the supermarket?
Clerk Kent.

Did you hear about what the artist liked to draw best?
His salary.

Did you hear about what the bus driver did with the thief?
She let him off.

Did you hear about the farmer who wrote dirty letters?
He used a pig pen.

4
All Work and No Play

What do you call an aged tailor?
An old sew-and-sew.

What's the hardest part of an astronaut's job?
Washing the (satellite) dishes.

Who is a good person to work at a hotel?
Someone who is inn-experienced.

How is the astronomer doing?
Things are looking up.

How is the archaeologist doing?
Her life's work is in ruins.

What do you get when you cross a boxer and a
photographer?
A striking resemblance.

How is the candy-maker doing?
So far he's making a mint.

Why did they go on strike at the mint?
They were making too much money.

Why did the secretary take a bikini to work?
She heard she was going in the typing pool.

What's the best way to lose your job writing obituaries?
Miss a deadline.

How do you fire a mailman?
Give him the sack.

Why would you go to the art gallery for a job?
They usually have a few openings.

How is the monogram business doing?
It's had some initial success.

What does the bicycle salesman do with bikes?
He peddles (pedals) them.

How do you find a writer in a crowded building?
Have him paged.

What happened to the novelist who was arrested?
He was printed and booked.

Why do marines eat so many apples?
They love the corps (core).

Anchors Aweigh

What kind of bird could join the navy?
  A carrier pigeon.

Where do they keep the kettle on a ship?
  In the boiler room.

What color is the ship's whistle?
  Navy blew (blue).

Why does the navy need so much money?
  *So the planes can land on a dime, and the
  sailors can sleep in their quarters.*

When is the best time to wash for dinner?
  When all hands are on deck.

What do sailors like in their soup?
  Crew-tons (croutons).

Army or Aren't We?

Where does the army hide its garbage?
In the mess tent.

What does the army do with priests?
It sends them on secret missions.

Where does the army keep its furs?
In foxholes.

Where did they put the psychic who joined the army?
On a trance-port (transport) ship.

Why did the two plumbers work together?
They were in sync (sink).

Why did the plumber decide to get married?
It was time he took the plunge-r.

Why did the weatherman measure the thermometer?
Because he wanted to know the fahren-height.

How did the weatherman get to work?
He hailed a cab.

Why was the mechanic in trouble?
For leaving oily (early).

How did the mechanic hear a secret?
The tires squealed.

What kind of ties do barbers wear?
Clip-ons.

What did the botanist say to the pine forest?
"Don't ever leave."

Why did the newspaperman keep a ruler on his desk?
So he could get his story straight.

Why can't you stay angry with an actress for very long?
Because she always makes-up.

What do you call the boss at a lumberyard?
The chairman of the boards.

What do you give a retired bus driver?
A token of appreciation.

How could you tell the tailor was tired?
His breath was coming in short pants.

What does it take to be a plumber?
Pipe dreams.

Why did the waiter fall over?
He was tipped.

5
Shop Till You Drop

How do you buy hammers?
By the pound.

How do you buy houses?
By the yard.

How do you buy grandparents?
By the gram.

How do you buy beds?
By the sack.

How do you buy lawyers?
By the case.

How do you buy men's socks?
Through the male (mail).

How do you buy a thief?
On the Home Shoplifting Channel.

How do you buy no-name items?
Anonymously.

Where do you buy doors?
At a dor-mitory.

Where do you buy a mink coat?
At a fur-niture store.

Where do electricians buy supplies?
At a factory outlet.

Where do you buy a comb?
At a parts store.

How does a little oven say hello?
With a micro-wave.

What kind of game can you play at a shopping center?
Price tag.

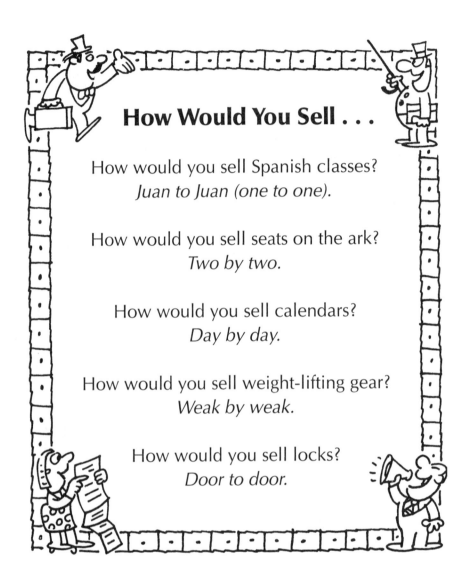

How Would You Sell . . .

How would you sell Spanish classes?
Juan to Juan (one to one).

How would you sell seats on the ark?
Two by two.

How would you sell calendars?
Day by day.

How would you sell weight-lifting gear?
Weak by weak.

How would you sell locks?
Door to door.

Why is the shopping so good in Hawaii?
There are isle after isle (aisle) of savings.

Why is the shopping so good in Mexico?
You only peso (pay-so) much.

Why didn't the actor like shopping?
He didn't have enough lines.

What was the biologist doing at the store?
He was looking for new genes (jeans).

Why did the biologist get a job at the store?
He really knew how to cell (sell).

What happened to the fighter at the shopping center?
He was malled (mauled).

How did the ex-convict get a job at the music store?
They found out he had a record.

Where do police shop?
At the department store.

What is the best place to do your taxes?
At the returns department.

Where do you bring lipstick that's not yours?
To the Glossed and Found.

Why did the woman have three hands on one arm?
She was wearing a watch.

What does a house wear in winter?
A coat of paint.

What does a royal octopus wear in winter?
A coat of arms.

What was the lazy coat doing in the closet?
Just hanging around.

What kind of underwear do horseback riders wear?
Jockey shorts.

What kind of hat do you wear on your leg?
A knee-cap.

Where do lobsters hang their wet laundry?
On a claws (clothes) line.

What do tropical fish wear on hot days?
Tank tops.

Why did Lassie's owner use Wisk?
*To get rid of the ring around
the collie.*

What frog pioneer wore a raccoon cap?
    Davy Croakett.

What department store did savage warriors shop in?
    Spears & Roebuck.

What did the Merry Men of Sherwood Forest wear to keep from getting wet?
    Robin hoods.

What did the little kid say after his shoes fell off?
    "If at first you don't succeed, tie, tie again."

What's the hardest foot to buy a shoe for?
    A square foot.

Why was the encyclopedia salesman so quiet?
Someone turned down the volume.

Why was the baseball player at the store?
For a sales pitch.

Why are they waving flyswatters in front of that building?
It's a shoo store.

What does the letter T put on when it gets dressed in the morning?
A T-shirt.

What is blue, tight-fitting and grants three wishes?
Designer jeanies (genies).

Why would you shop for a car in Las Vegas?
They have so many dealers.

What did the duck say to the clerk?
"Put this on my bill."

What should you give a monkey for his birthday?
An ape recorder.

What do you call a dog at the stereo shop?
A woofer.

What do you call a little bird at the stereo shop?
A tweeter.

How did the dove save so much money?
By using coooo-pons (coupons).

What makeup does Mary Poppins wear?
Super-calla-fraga-lipstick.

Why was the lifeguard at the store?
He heard he could save a lot.

Why was the fruit stand empty?
It hadn't been re-peared (repaired).

At the store, what do you say after they say "hello"?
"Good buy."

6
School Days

Did you hear about the witch who was kicked out of school?

> *She was ex-spelled (expelled).*

When is it correct to say "I is"?
> *"I is the letter after H."*

How do you find a math tutor?
> *Place an add (ad).*

Hairy!

SUE: What are you going to do after hairdressing school?

BEA: I plan on looking for permanent work.

SUE: What do hairdressers do on their days off?

BEA: Curl up with a good book.

What happened when the banker missed a day of school?
He brought a note.

Why did you need a reservation at the library?
It was booked-up.

Did you hear about the pitcher at school?
He was graded on a curve.

Why did the historian read books on the ancient Greeks?
It was his favorite past-time.

How do astrologers talk to each other?
In sign language.

What subject are you taking in school when you write all over a map?

Geo-graffiti.

What bug gets the best marks in math?

An arithme-tick.

Where do you read the most boring articles?

In a snooze-paper.

In what newspaper column did President Lincoln give advice on life and love?

"Dear Abey."

What do students hate to study for?

De-tests.

What tests does Count Dracula study for?

Blood tests.

Where do algebra teachers soak after a long hard day?
In a math tub.

What do math teachers eat from?
Multiplication tables.

What donuts can't pass a math test?
Flunkin' Donuts.

Where do geometry teachers go on Friday nights?
Square dancing.

What's a geometry teacher's favorite place in New York City?
Times Square.

Where Do You Go?

Where do you go to become a prisoner?
Go directly to Yale.

Where do you go to become a telephone operator?
A call-ege (college).

Where do you go to learn how to joust?
Knight school.

Where do you go to learn how to start fires?
Tinder-garten.

Where do you go to become a Spanish teacher?
Señor high.

Where do you go to become an astrologer?
A universe-ity.

7
The Zany Zoo

What swims and has six pockets?
A pool shark.

What do llamas like to eat?
Lleaves and llettuce.

What is striped and then spotted?
A zebra that's been seen.

What is both large and small at the same time?
A jumbo shrimp.

Hop To It

Did you hear about the quiet frog?
> *He never said a word till the day he croaked.*

What happens if you swallow a frog?
> *You could croak at any minute.*

When is a car like a frog?
> *When it's being toad (towed).*

What would you get if you crossed Moby Dick and a Timex?
> *A whale watch-er.*

Why was the tuna so sad about his wife?
> *He lobster, and couldn't flounder.*

What do you call 300 rabbits marching backwards?
> *A receding hare line.*

How much did the polar bear weigh?
  A ton-dra (tundra).

What do you call a parrot in a raincoat?
  Polly-unsaturated.

What kind of fisherman always cries?
  A whaler (wailer).

What do you say to a crying whale?
  "Quit your blubbering."

How does a whale walk?
  Eel toe, eel toe, eel toe.

What makes an elk feel good after it eats too much?
Elk-a-Seltzer.

Where does Bullwinkle go for a roller coaster ride?
To an a-moose-ment park.

Why doesn't the deer cross the road up ahead?
Because the buck always stops here.

What dance do deer do?
The doe-si-doe.

What do you call a reindeer who refuses to pull Santa's sleigh?
Unemployed.

What do you offer an alligator to eat?
Anything he wants.

What do alligators do when you give them some string?
They floss after they eat.

Why don't alligators ride bicycles?
Their feet are too short to reach the pedals.

What do they call dinosaurs south of Texas?
Tyrannosaurus Mex.

Why won't anyone sleep in the same room as that dinosaur?
Because it's a brontosnorus.

Why do elephants dance minuets?
Because they don't know how to watlz.

What do you call two elephants walking on tiptoes?
Sneakers.

What do you give a nervous elephant?
Trunkquilizers.

What's pretty, gray, has a trunk and wears glass slippers?
Cinderelephant.

How do you know there is an elephant in your backpack?
Because you can't close it up.

What is as large as an elephant but weighs nothing?
Its shadow.

What is the highest form of animal life?
  The giraffe.

What did the giraffe sing to the donkey?
  "I've got you under my chin."

Do giraffes go to church?
  Yes, they attend High Mass.

What's worse than a giraffe with a soar throat?
  A centipede with corns.

What newspaper do giraffes read?
  "The Tall Street Journal."

What would you get if you crossed a giraffe with a pit bull?
  A dog that barks at airplanes.

Why did they give the bride a turtle and an antelope?
So she could have something old and something gnu.

What magazine features animals on the cover?
Gnusweek (Newsweek).

Did you hear about the sleepy king of the beasts?
He was lion down.

Who cuts the lion's hair?
His mane man.

How do you make an elephant fly?
Buy a long enough zipper.

What do you call a fly with no wings?
   A walk.

What do you call a deer with no eyes?
   No-eye deer (idea).

What would you get if you crossed a hyena with an elephant?
   An animal that never forgets a joke.

What would you get if you crossed a hyena with a vampire?
   An animal that laughs at the sight of blood.

What would you get if you crossed a hyena with a parrot?
   An animal that tells you what he's laughing at.

Why did Santa only have seven reindeer on Christmas Eve?
Because Comet stayed home to clean the kitchen.

What did the mother dinosaur say to hurry her baby along?
Pronto, Saurus.

What is yellow, green, blue, black, red, orange, purple, brown and gray?
A hippo holding a box of crayons.

What would you get if you crossed a hippo with a pigeon?
A bird that breaks a lot of telephone wires.

What's large, gray and stamps out forest fires?
Smokey the Hippo.

How do you know there was a hippo in your refrigerator?
He carved his initials in the butter.

8
Young MacDonald's Farm

Did you hear about the cow that couldn't give milk?
She thought she was an udder failure.

What did the cow say to the bull in the car?
"I'll drive, you steer."

What is the cow's favorite song?
"Moooo-n River."

How do chickens type?
With the hunt and peck system.

Which is smarter, a chicken or a canary?
Have you ever heard of Kentucky Fried Canary?

Which side of a chicken has the most feathers?
The outside.

Why did the chicken cross the ski slope?
To get to the other slide.

What would you get if you crossed a poodle with a chicken?
Pooched eggs.

What kind of cars do chickens drive?
Yolkswagens.

Who is a pig's favorite artist?
Pigasso.

Where do pigs take their laundry?
To the hog wash.

Where do pigs go on vacation?
Hamsterdam.

What position do pigs play on a baseball team?
Short-slop.

Where do pigs sleep in Alaska?
In pigloos.

What kind of vehicles do pigs drive?
Pig-up trucks.

Chicken Feed

How much do they pay chickens for their eggs?
A poultry (paltry) sum.

Why do chickens need vacations?
Because they're cooped up all day.

Why do roosters crow?
Because crows roost.

What did the farmer say when he saw three ducks in his mailbox?
"Bills, bills, bills."

Are potatoes good drivers?
When they keep their eyes peeled.

Where do they keep all the pigs in Idaho?
In the state pen.

How do you fix a hole in the garden?
With a vegetable patch.

How do baby sheep stay cool in the summer?
They use a lamb-shade.

Why did the farmer's wife think no one listened to her?
Only the sheep herd-her (herder).

What do you call a cow that can't do anything right?
Miss-steak.

What do you say to a sleeping vegetable gardener?
"Rest in peas (peace)."

Why did Mickey Mouse go into outer space?
He was looking for Pluto.

What kind of truck do they haul pigs in?
An 18-squealer.

How do you get a sick pig to the hospital?
Call a hambulance.

Why did the skunk spray the courtroom?
The judge said, "Odor in the Court."

What do you rub on your sick pig?
Oinkment.

What would you get if you crossed a pig with a centipede?
Bacon and legs.

What would you get if you crossed a cow with a backyard?
A lawn mooer.

What is a cow's favorite movie?
"The Sound of Moosic."

What do cows wear in Hawaii?
Moo-moos.

What do they call little black and white cats in Denmark?
Kittens.

Why won't they let some cats play cards?
Because they're cheetahs.

What's the difference between a cat and a bullfrog?
A cat has nine lives, but a frog croaks every night.

If you cross a frog with a hare, what will it say?
"Rabbit, rabbit."

What does a frog say while polishing silver?
"Rub it, rub it"

What happened when the frog's van broke down on the turnpike?
It was toad away.

What do frogs do for the CIA?
Croak-and-dagger stuff.

How do cats make phone calls?
They call Persian to Persian.

What is black and white and has 16 wheels?
A dalmatian on roller skates.

What dog is the best flier?
An air-dale.

What kind of dog likes corn on the cob?
A Husk-y.

What is black and white and red all over?
A dalmatian with a sunburn.

What's a dog's favorite cheese?
Muttzarella (mozzarella).

If you meet a mad dog, what steps should you take?
>*Very, very large ones.*

Why did you cut down the dogwood tree?
>*I didn't like its bark.*

What would you get if you crossed a dog with a potted plant?
>*A fidodendron.*

What would you get if you crossed a Doberman with Lassie?
>*A dog that chews off your leg and then runs for help.*

What dog catches criminals?
>*A copper spaniel.*

What would you get if you crossed a racing dog with a bee?
A greyhound buzz.

What would happen if you crossed a pit bull with a yappy poodle?
You'd get a vicious gossip.

What kind of dog likes air conditioning?
A hot dog.

What barks more, a collie or an Irish setter?
It's about arf and arf.

What is the most expensive dog?
A golden retriever.

How did the dog feel about his flea collar?
It ticked him off.

What is a dalmatian's favorite sports magazine?
"Spots Illustrated."

What would you get if you crossed a Doberman and a giraffe?
A watchdog for the 6th floor.

What kind of shoes do dog trainers wear?
Hush puppies.

What kind of motorcycle do dogs buy?
>*Houndas.*

What do you call a horse that never stops telling you what to do?
>*A real nag.*

What was the horse doing at the stock market?
>*Bucking the trends.*

How can you make a flower say something?
>*There are vase to make it s-talk.*

What do you call the man who sprays the flowers?
>*"Mist-er."*

Why do frogs go to baseball games?
They like to catch flies.

What would you get if you crossed a groundhog with a catcher's mitt?
Six more weeks of baseball.

Did you hear about the lawn mower that went on the stage?
It had a scrapbook full of clippings.

What did the blacksmith say to the runaway horse?
"Stop or I'll shoe-it (shoot)."

Did you hear about the corn farmer who joined the army?
He wanted to be a kernel (colonel).

How did the cowboy break his leg in the rodeo?
>*They gave him a bum steer.*

What's 200 feet tall, weighs 20,000 pounds and eats tin cans?
>*Goatzilla.*

What is green and gray and has a lot of whiskers?
>*A seasick goat.*

What do you call twelve ducks in a carton?
>*A box of quackers.*

What does a male duck buy to wear to the prom?
>*A ducksedo.*

What do mice wear playing basketball?
>*Squeakers.*

What is a Texas bull's favorite saying?
Remember the Alamoo.

Where do frogs keep their coats?
In the croakroom.

What would you get if you crossed a frog with a distant planet?
Star warts.

What did one frog say to the other frog?
"Time's fun when you're having flies."

What do frogs order at the diner?
French flies and a large croak.

9
Stars On Parade!

Why did the Hollywood chicken cross the road?
To see Gregory Peck.

Where was Solomon's temple?
On the side of his head.

What is the difference between Madonna and a mouse?
One charms the he's, the other harms the cheese.

How can you tell Madonna buys most of her clothes on sale?

Because they are often half-off.

What do Kermit the Frog and Mack the Knife have in common?

The same middle name.

What do you say when you want Dolly's attention?

"Parton me."

Do you know what Mr. Goodyear is doing now?

He is re-tired.

Why didn't the king and queen potato want their daughter to marry the anchorman?

Because he was just a common-tator (commentator).

Silly Cash Stash

Where does Jack Frost keep all his money?
In a slush fund.

How did Old Man River lose all his money?
He got soaked.

Where do kittens get their money from?
Pet-ty cash.

Where does Mother Nature keep her money?
In a cloud bank.

Where does a track star keep his money?
In a pole vault.

How did we find out about the goose that laid the golden egg?

Both Jack and the beans-talk (beanstalk).

Why was Roy Rogers always smiling and shooting his gun?
He was Trigger happy.

What do you say to a silent movie star?
"You should be scene and not heard."

Why can't bad actors fish?
They never remember their lines.

What did the mighty Samson do when his son grew a pony tail?
He cut his heir.

Let's Make-Up

How do you glue your mouth shut?
With lipstick.

Who do you call if your lipstick gets sick?
A cos-medic (cosmetic).

What happened to the lady who stole some eye make-up?
She got fifty lashes.

How do they ship cosmetics?
On an eye liner.

Why did the comedian get a job at the beauty shop?
So he could make-up some new jokes.

Did you hear about the lady who chewed her nails?
She polished off all of them.

Where does Superman go bowling?
At Lois Lanes.

What happened when Santa took boxing lessons?
He decked the halls.

Who brings gifts to the dentist's office?
Santa Floss.

What's the difference between a knight and Rudolph?
One is a dragon slayer, the other is a sleigh dragger.

Where does Santa keep his suit?
In the Claus-it (closet).

Why didn't Mata Hari ever smile?
She was no laughing Mata.

Did Adam and Eve ever have a date?
No, just an apple.

What is tasty and a great inventor?
Marconi and cheese.

Where does Snow White keep her yacht?
At any of her seven dwarfs (wharfs).

Where is Captain Hook's treasure chest?
Under his treasure shirt.

Who hasn't done his ironing in years?
Wrinkle Stilskin.

Did you know most of King Arthur's men had insomnia?
It was one sleepless knight after another.

What does the Lone Ranger's horse eat with?
Silverware.

Why do horses float down the river on their backs?
So they won't get their shoes wet.

Where do horses go on their honeymoon?
Niagara Stalls.

What kind of cars do Santa's elves drive?
Toyotas.

Who sings and helps Santa?
Elves Presley.

Where does Saint Nick go on holidays?
Santa Cruz.

Where does Mrs. Claus go on holidays?
Santa Fe.

Did you hear about the invisible Santa?
You can't see him, but you can feel his presents.

10
Games People Play

What game do birds like to play?
Hide and beak.

What game do you play with bees?
Hive and seek.

What game can you play while the earth is shaking?
Quakes and ladders.

What is a baker's favorite game?
Tic Tac Dough.

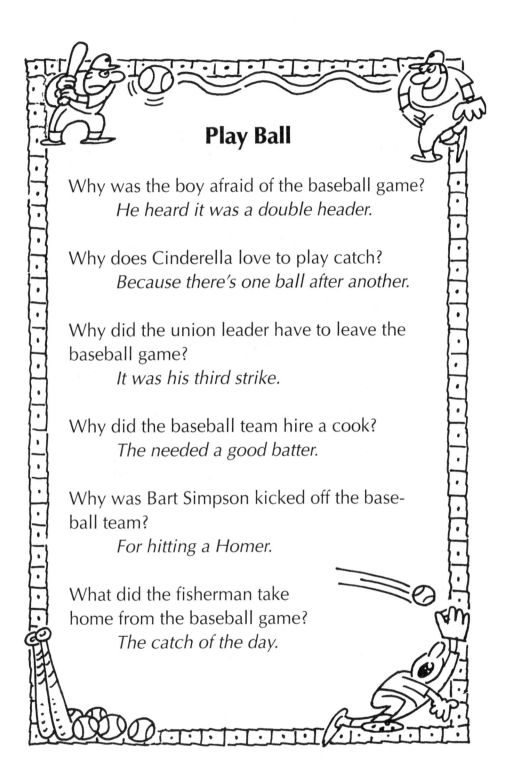

Play Ball

Why was the boy afraid of the baseball game?
He heard it was a double header.

Why does Cinderella love to play catch?
Because there's one ball after another.

Why did the union leader have to leave the baseball game?
It was his third strike.

Why did the baseball team hire a cook?
The needed a good batter.

Why was Bart Simpson kicked off the baseball team?
For hitting a Homer.

What did the fisherman take home from the baseball game?
The catch of the day.

How did the football player get into the theatre for free?
He received a pass.

What did the fisherman take to the football game?
His tackle.

Where does your mother's mother sit at the ballgame?
In the grand-stand.

Why did the boxer change his socks?
He could smell de-feet (defeat).

How did the bus driver lose the game?
He missed his turn.

Why did the runner bring his barber to the Olympics?
He wanted to shave a few seconds off his time.

What did the silly swimmer do with his Olympic gold medal?
He had it bronzed.

How do people in San Francisco watch the Olympics?
On cable-cars.

How did the fisherman watch the Olympics?
On a net-work.

How did the cook watch the Olympics?
On the dish.

How did Mrs. Goodyear watch the Olympics?
On the tube.

11
Pros and Cons

What did the artist say in court?
"This painting was framed."

Did you hear about the proud prisoner?
He was taught never to be ashamed of his convictions.

What do bank robbers like with their soup?
Safe crackers.

What kind of telephones do convicts prefer?
Cell-ular phones.

What is the best thing about being a sick thief?
You can always take something for it.

Why should you never interrupt a fat judge while he's eating?
There's too much at steak.

How do we know that Al Capone had venetian blinds?
Otherwise, it would have been curtains for him.

Did you hear about the shoplifter at the lingerie shop?
She gave police the slip.

Did you hear about the convict who was allergic to jail?
He would break-out in hives.

Did you hear about the short psychic who escaped from jail?
A small medium at large.

Did you hear about the thief at the butcher shop?
He jumped on the scale and gave himself a weigh (away).

Why did the mob want to kill Einstein?
He knew too much.

Did you hear about the guy who stole the judge's calendar?
He got twelve months.

What did the witch say after the California plane was cancelled?
"There's no west for the wicked."

What did the grateful iceberg say to the *Titanic*?
"Sank you very much."

What did the *Titanic* want from its boss?
A raise.

All Creatures Great & Small

What space creature comes from the dryer?
The static Kling-on.

What creatures are the best at trivia games?
Little gnome facts.

What beast comes from the vegetable garden?
The creature from the black legume.

What creature comes from Canada?
The Toronto-saurus.

What did the prisoner say to the judge?
"Pardon me."

Why was Doctor Jekyll so hard to find?
He knew how to Hyde.

Why was the weatherman arrested?
For shooting the breeze.

What kind of lotion do monsters wear at the beach?
Sunscream.

Who wrote the monster's favorite book?
A ghost writer.

What kind of glasses do monsters drink from?
Franken-steins.

How does a werewolf brush its hairy mouth?
With a fine tooth comb.

Where do jewellers go on vacation?
On sapphire-i (safari).

What happened when the seats in all the police cars were stolen?

> *Police had nothing to go on.*

What happened to the guy who stole 300 O'Henrys?
> *He ended up behind bars.*

Did you hear about the slow composer?
> *He ended up behind bars too.*

What happened to the retired bartender?
> *He's no longer behind bars.*

What prison did they send the canary to?
> *Sing Sing.*

Why was the clock in prison?
> *It was just doing time.*

12
Quick Snappers

Bad spellers untie!

Catching a Sasquatch would be a big feat.

"Hopefully, this water is from a wishing well."

"My job at the phone company is really taking its toll."

Did you hear about the board (bored) carpenter?

"Does the name Pavlov ring a bell?"

Wouldn't It Be Funny If . . .

A dressmaker slipped.

A logger fell.

A painter got new shades.

A surfer waved.

A dentist had a fire drill.

A tennis player needed a match.

A quarterback passed out.

A jockey felt hoarse.

A bridge had a toll-free number.

A dry cleaner was pressed for time.

The Doubtful Dictionary

Naval Destroyer:
> *A hula hoop with a nail in it.*

Penmanship:
> *What writers use to cross the ocean.*

Writer's block:
> *Where all the writers live.*

Wine glasses:
> *What near-sighted complainers wear.*

Silver screen:
> *What rich sunbathers wear.*

Bacteria:
> *The far end of a cafeteria.*

Did you hear about the carpenter who was nailed for speeding?

You Said It!

"If the cab ride is free it's not fare."

"Expensive tissue is nothing to sneeze at."

"Boiling an egg for three minutes isn't hard."

"Total eclipses scare the daylights out of me."

"Sir Lancelot loved knight life."

"Masseurs are people who knead people."

"Clones are people two."

"Pharmacists are the pill-ars of society."

Did you hear about the human cannonball who couldn't be fired?

Did you hear about the human cannonball who was lost?
It was tough to find a man of his caliber.

How do Eskimos stick together?
With i-glue (igloo).

Why did the three pigs leave home?
Their father was a boar.

What is the potato's favorite song?
"I Only Have Eyes for You."

What's a mouse's favorite game?
Hide-and-Squeak.

How can you avoid being driven crazy?
Walk!

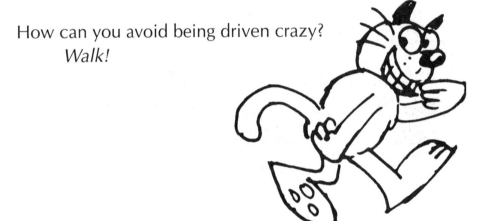

13
Eat Your Heart Out

What do you say to an octopus at the dinner table?
> *"Get your elbow elbow elbow elbow elbow off the table."*

What do you say to a liar at the dinner table?
> *"Pass the baloney."*

What do you say to a politician at the dinner table?
> *"Pass the buck, please."*

What is the difference between a banana and a bell?
You can only peel the banana once.

What is Big Foot's favorite food?
Sas-squash.

What does a rich ham wear?
Designer cloves.

What did the scientist say when he found a 200-year-old sausage?
"I found the missing link."

Why was the fat politician so happy about his weight?
He was gaining in the polls.

What's the difference between a gullible person and a pizza?
One's easy to cheat, the other's cheesy to eat.

What is an Eskimos's favorite food?
Iceberg-ers (burgers).

What is a singer's favorite food?
Tune-a-sandwiches.

What do you get when you cross a spaceship and a chef?
A flying sauce-r.

How do you cook an alligator?
In a crock pot.

Where do astronauts cook their food?
On a space wok (walk).

How do you catch celery?
You stalk it.

How do you weigh fish?
On a scale of one to ten.

Why can't two waiters play tennis?
They'll both want to serve.

Why were the ice cream and the fudge sauce all alone?
The banana split.

Serving Your Fellow Man

Why won't most cannibals eat clowns?
>*They taste funny.*

Did you hear about the cannibal who was late for dinner?
>*They gave him the cold shoulder.*

Did you hear about the cannibal who ate his mother-in-law?
>*She didn't agree with him.*

Did you hear about the cannibal wedding reception?
>*They toasted the bride, and then they toasted the groom.*

Did you hear about the two cannibals who ordered "The Man From Prague?"
>*They decided to split the Czech.*

What does Charlie Brown like on his toast?
Peanuts butter.

How did the comedian like his eggs?
Funny side up.

Did you hear about the smart cook?
He always used his noodle.

Why did the ice cream cone surrender?
He knew when he was licked.

What does a baby kangaroo have for breakfast?
Pouched (poached) eggs.

Corny Flakes

What vegetable do you throw away the outside, cook the inside, eat the outside and throw away the inside?
> *Corn on the cob.*

What is a monster's favorite cereal?
> *Dreaded Wheat.*

What did the thief have for breakfast?
> *Hot coffee.*

What do monkeys eat in the morning?
> *The breakfast of chimp-ions.*

What does a policeman like on his toast?
> *Traffic jam.*

What does Santa have for breakfast?
> *Snow flakes.*

Did you hear about the bread that never went bad?
After they made it they broke the mould (mold).

What kind of shoes do bakers wear?
Loafers.

Why did the baker take a raisin out to a movie?
He didn't have a date.

Why did the baker quit making donuts?
He hated the whole business.

How much does Chinese soup weigh?
About won-ton (one ton).

What TV show do you watch after eating Chinese food?
Wheel of Fortune cookies.

14
Is There A Doctor In The House?

What did the doctor say to the Incredible Shrinking Man?
"You'll just have to be a little patient."

Which eye gets hit the most?
A bull's-eye.

Moaners & Groaners

What was the *Titanic* shivering for?
    It was a nervous wreck.

What kind of person was the captain of the *Titanic*?
    Deep down he was a nice guy.

What do liars do after they die?
    Lie still.

What has no lungs or kidneys, but has thirteen hearts?
    A deck of cards.

What did one casket say to the other casket?
    "Is that you coffin (coughin')?"

Did you hear about the sad pillow?
    It was a little down.

Where did the psychiatrist like to go for a walk?
Along the psychopath.

Why didn't the dentist ask his secretary on a date?
He was already taking out a tooth.

How did the dentist break his mirror?
Acci-dentally.

What did the dentist see at the North Pole?
Molar Bears.

What does The Dentist Of The Year get?
A little plaque.

What does a dentist do on a roller coaster?
He braces himself.

What game did the dentist play as a child?
    Caps and robbers.

Why did the doctor get such a big dog?
    He always wanted a lab assistant.

What is a doctor's favorite musical instrument?
    An ear drum.

Did you hear about the doctor who golfed in the dark?
    He liked swinging nightclubs.

What was the doctor doing in the fridge?
    Fixing a cold cut sandwich.

Why did Zeus and Apollo hang out at the health club?
They were both myth-fits.

How does a funeral home get rid of ashes?
The old fashioned way: They urn them.

How do you get to the morgue?
Turn left at the coroner.

How did the psychologist change his flat?
With de-spair (the spare) tire.

Why did the doctor return his dog to the pet store?
It wouldn't heel (heal).

What kind of mouthwash do doctors recommend?
Stetho-Scope.

Did you hear about the frustrated dietician?
His patience was wearing thin.

What did the man say after his
knee operation?
"I stand corrected."

15
Tuff Stuff

Who fixes the president's teeth?
   The presi-dentist.

What kind of shampoo does the president use?
   Hair Force One.

Where does the president wipe his feet?
   On a diplo-mat.

Where does the ambassador fish?
   In the embass-sea (embassy).

What were the nylons doing in Washington, D.C.?
The were running for Congress.

How did the Congressman get a son?
He adopted a Bill.

How cold was it yesterday?
It was so cold a politician had his hands in his own pockets.

Where does the British government keep its teacups?
In the Cabinet.

What did the king and queen of hearts do on their daughter's birthday?
They sent her a card.

When do clocks die?
When their time is up.

Why was the aquarium depressed?
It lacked porpoise.

What is the worst part of snorkling?
It's a tank-less job.

What could cause a lot of trouble
if it stopped smoking?
A chimney.

What got the gutters in trouble?
Eaves dropping on the neighbors.

What got the house in trouble?
Siding with the neighbors.

What got the wall in trouble?
Being plastered.

What got the plywood in trouble?
Coming unglued.

Who do you take hunting for a frozen dinner?
A TV Guide.

What happened when the plaid army met the striped army?
They clashed.

What would you get if you crossed a lawyer with a tailor?
A suit case.

What would you get if you crossed a math teacher with a tennis player?
A numbers racquet.

What would you get if you crossed a taxidermist with a Big Mac?
Stuffed.

What color do you always think you've seen before?
Déjà-blue (déjà vu).

What has twelve legs and two wings?
A hockey team.

What holds up the roof of a newspaper?
Gossip columns.

What is blue and a fake?
An artificial smurf.

16
Believe It or Nuts

How do angels greet each other?
They wave halo.

What does a one-legged turkey say?
"Hobble, hobble."

What title did the pretty boa constrictor win?
"Hiss Universe."

How do baby fish know how to swim?
Finstinct.

What car runs under water?
A Scubaru.

What sea serpent solves mysteries?
Sher-lochness Holmes.

Who was the meanest octopus in the Old West?
Billy the Squid.

Who is the fastest detective?
Quick Tracy.

Who is the most forgetful detective?
Dick Spacy.

Who's the meanest ape?
Gorilla the Hun.

Who's the meanest chicken?
Atilla the Hen.

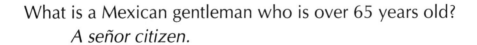

What chickens rob people?
Peck-pockets.

What is a Mexican gentleman who is over 65 years old?
A señor citizen.

What do babies love to listen to?
Rock-a-bye 'n' roll music.

What do depressed cheerleaders suffer from?
The sis-boom-blahs.

What Jedi loves winter sports?
Luke Ski-walker.

What pain do many composers suffer from?
Bach-aches.

What songs bore people so much that they fall asleep without even trying?
Dull-abies.

What would you get if you crossed a hen with a four-leaf clover?

A good-cluck charm.

What's a tyrant's favorite drink?

Cruel-Aid.

What's Scrooge's favorite drink?

Gruel-Aid.

What camera develops underwater pictures immediately?

A Poolaroid.

Where do mice park their boats?

At the hickory dickory dock.

What would you get if you crossed an Orca family with a jeep?

A vehicle with 4-whale dive.

Why don't bananas like to sun bathe?

They have a tendency to peel.

What's the tallest plant in France?

The Eiffel Flower.

What did the catcher put outside his front door?

A welcome mitt.

What would you get if you crossed a baby with a yogi?
A goo-gooru.

What would you get if you crossed a klutz with a hitch-hiker?
A hobo who's all thumbs.

What does the victim of a practical joke send the person who pulled it?
A prank (thank) you note.

Where does Ziggy keep his allowance?
In a Ziggybank.

What would you get if you crossed a bear with a puppy?
Winnie-the-Pooch.

Why did the blue jay get a perm?
Because the curly bird catches the worm.

Why did the little bird buy the big bird a greeting card?
For Feather's (Father's) Day.

Who do birds marry?
Their tweethearts.

Why did the mother parrot scold the baby parrot?
For not talking back.

What's the difference between an airplane and a chicken?
An airplane doesn't have any meat on its wing.

What do grouchy people fly in?
Com-planes.

What is the largest meteorite?
Whaley's Comet.

What do sneakers do when they're angry?
Stick their tongues out.

What is a zombie's favorite sport?
Hearseback riding.

What's a little zombie's favorite stuffed animal?
Its deady (teddy) bear.

What game do little ghouls like to play?
Corpse (Cops) and Robbers.

Why did the TV producer go to the doctor?
To have his cast removed.

Why wouldn't the vampire climb back into his coffin at sunrise?
He was an all-day sucker.

Why did the rich parents keep their son in the refrigerator?
So he wouldn't get spoiled.

If a mouse ran out of your stove and you had a gun, could you shoot it?
No, it would be out of your range.

What do you get when you use soap and water on the stove?
Foam on the range.

What invention allows people to walk through walls?
Doors.

What stays indoors no matter how many times you put it out?
The light.

What did the digital watch say to its mother?
"Look, Ma, no hands!"

What were Alexander Graham Bell's first words?
"Goo-goo."

17
Animal Crackers

What bear never wants to grow up?
Peter Pan-da.

What is the most boring farm animal?
Blah, blah, black sheep.

What is the meanest farm animal?
The bullygoat.

What is the busiest farm animal?
The mouse. It's always in a scurry.

What would you get if you crossed Chicken Little with Kermit?

> *A frog that peeps as it leaps.*

What do you call a crazy frog?

> *A croakpot.*

What would you get if you crossed a giraffe with a polar bear?

> *An animal that wouldn't mind cold weather if it could get a long enough scarf.*

How do geese communicate with headquarters?

> *Over squawkie-talkies.*

Where do you find the names of famous owls?
In "Whoooo's Who."

Where do owls go to dance?
Hootenannies.

What kind of books do owls like?
Mostly whoo-done-its.

Why are spiders good doctors?
They make house crawls.

Which is most feared—the hawk, the lion, or the skunk?
The grizzly bear. He ate all three, hawk, lion and stinker.

What do little monkeys eat at nap time?
Chocolate chimp cookies.

What do you call an animal with two humps that wades in the ocean?
A wet camel.

How do you keep a camel from going through the eye of a needle?
Tie a knot in its tail.

Why did the elephant visit the bathing suit department?
He wanted to see something new in trunks.

What would you get if you crossed a skunk with Sprint?
A telephone that you hold up to your ear but away from your nose.

Why aren't moles welcome in banks?
Because they burrow too much.

How is a rubber band like a crocodile?
If you pull it too hard, it snaps.

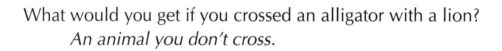

What would you get if you crossed an alligator with a rooster?
"Croc-a-doodle-do!"

What would you get if you crossed an alligator with a lion?
An animal you don't cross.

What would you get if you crossed an alligator with a pygmy?
A crocodile with a short temper.

How do you get a crocodile on a roller coaster?
Buy him a ticket.

How do you get a crocodile into a fine restaurant?
In a shirt and tie.

What did the snake give his girlfriend when he escorted her home?
A hiss goodnight.

Where do you gas up a horse?
At a filly (filling) station.

Where do cowboys go to ride horses and be impolite?
To a rude-eo.

What prehistoric creature is huge, yellow, and shaped like a lemon?
A dino-sour.

What do you call a brontosaurus who gets angry when he doesn't win?
A saur (sore) loser.

What dog is always carrying shopping bags?
A German Shlepherd.

What would you get if you crossed a German shepherd with a kid wearing braces?
A dog whose bark is worse than his overbite.

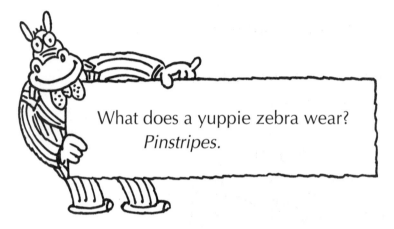

What does a yuppie zebra wear?
Pinstripes.

What famous cow wore a feather headdress and smoked a peace pipe?
Geronimoo.

What does Porky do to keep himself busy?
Pigsaw puzzles.

What would you get if you crossed a rhinoceros with a snowflake?
I don't know, but you'd better watch out for blizzard conditions.

How do skunks know when to release their terrible smell?
Instink.

What would you get if you crossed a cheetah with a centipede?

A wildcat that loves to run, but takes too long to put on its sneakers.

What would you get if you crossed a salmon with a tadpole?

A frog that swims upstream before it croaks.

When do little gnus chew the furniture?

When they're gnaw-ty.

Santa's Little Deers

Where do you find the names of Santa's reindeer?
In "Hooves' Who."

Which one of Santa's reindeer sells hats?
Haber-Dasher.

Which one of Santa's reindeer does concerts?
Ma-Donner.

What happens to a rhinoceros' armor when it stays out in the rain too long?
It rhinocerusts.

What is yellowish brown and wears a mask?
The Lone Lion.

Name two famous animals with the same middle name.
Elsa the Lioness and Jumbo the Elephant.

What is the most squeamish animal?
An ele-faint.

What do you give a nervous elephant?
   Trunkquilizers.

What would you get if you crossed a PC with an elephant?
   Lots more memory.

What would you get if you crossed an eagle with an elephant?
   A two-ton bird that likes to fly but has trouble landing.

What would you get if you crossed a dog with an elephant?
   I don't know, but you'd better watch out when it jumps on your bed.

What would you get if you crossed a rattlesnake with a dog?

> *A puppy whose bite is MUCH worse than its bark.*

What's a dog's favorite sport?

> *Biscuit-ball.*

What kind of dog does Count Dracula have?

> *A bloodhound.*

What kind of dog does Noah have?

> *A floodhound.*

What dogs pick out furniture?

> *In-terrier decorators.*

What do you say when you tickle a puppy?

> *"Poochie, poochie, coo."*

18
The Show Must Go!

Where can you watch *Gone With the Wind* 24 hours a day?
  On Gable TV.

What does a comedian say when he sticks his tongue out in a doctor's office?
  "H-ahhhh."

Why won't television ever take the place of newspapers?
  You can't wrap fish in a television.

What's a ghoul's favorite musical instrument?
The spook-ulele.

What duet do police officers play on the piano?
Cop sticks.

What duet do butchers play on the piano?
Chop steaks (sticks).

How did the composer sneak into the opera house?
Through the Bach door.

What do the children of classical musicians like to listen to?
Bach 'n' roll.

What's a Jedi's favorite musical instrument?
The Luk-ulele.

Which band plays the loudest music?
A band of gorillas.

What's a rock star's favorite car?
A Rock 'n' Rolls-Royce.

What did the band play at the crooked politician's wedding?
"Here Comes the Bribe."

Where do turkeys go when they want to dance?
To the Fowl Ball.

What is a concert musician's favorite dessert?
Cello pudding.

What do musicians play in a judge's office?
Chamber music.

What kind of bird loves punk music?
A mo-hawk.

What rock group steals their instruments?
A band of thieves.

What is a foot doctor's favorite song?
"There's No Business Like Toe Business."

What is a ski instructor's favorite song?
"There's No Business Like Snow Business."

What is a plumber's favorite song?
"Singing in the Drain."

What is a flute player's favorite number?
Fife (five).

What does Tarzan play on in the playground?
The jungle gym

Who gave the Ghost of Christmas Past a cold?
Ebe-sneezer Scrooge.

Who does Curious George become when he's angry?
Furious George.

What rock group is made up of a lead singer and three chickens?
Gladys Knight and the Peeps.

What sourpuss watches TV all the time?
A grouch potato.

Who sits in front of the TV with bad posture?
A slouch potato.

What little kangaroo watches TV all day long?
A pouch potato.

What's a pickle's favorite game show?
"Let's Make a Dill (Deal)."

What does Bullwinkle sing every December 25th?
Christmoose carols.

Where do candy-coated chocolates perform music videos?
On M & M TV.

When is holding on the phone like doing a trapeze act?
When you're hanging on.

What daytime dramas do dummies watch?
Dope operas.

What kind of bird likes ballet music?
A cockatutu.

What is Benji's favorite ballet music?
"The Muttcracker Suite."

What musical instrument did the Old Woman Who Lived in a Shoe play?
The shoehorn.

What would you get if you crossed an anchorman with a pair of underwear?

News briefs.

Does Fred Flintstone draw?

Sort of—he yabba, dabba, doo-dles.

What did Mervin the Magician say when he couldn't find the rabbit he put in the hat?

"Hare today, gone tomorrow."

19
Mad Mottos and Screwy Slogans

What's a gardener's motto?
A peony saved is a peony earned.

What's a barber's motto?
Hairy today, gone tomorrow.

What's a con artist's motto?
Cheat, drink, and be merry.

What's a justice of the peace's motto?
Eat, drink, and be married.

What's a bigamist's motto?
The more the marrieder.

What's a sculptor's motto?
All work and no clay makes Jack a dull boy.

What's Rapunzel's motto?
Easy comb, easy grow.

What's Kleenex's motto?
*Sneezy come,
sneezy go.*

What's a sheep herder's motto?
Shear and shear alike.

What's a skunk's motto?
Eat, stink, and be merry.

What's the marathon winner's motto?
He who hesitates is last.

What's the Tinman's motto?
Oil's well that ends well.

What's Pinocchio's motto?
No nose is good nose.

What's a witch's motto?
Demons (diamonds) are a ghoul's (girl's) best friend.

What's a hockey player's motto?
The puck stops here.

What's a boxer's motto?
If at fist you don't succeed, try, try again.

What's a sheep's motto?
All's wool that ends wool.

What's a soap company's motto?
Grime does not pay.

What's a blizzard's motto?
The snow must go on.

What's Jonah's motto?
All's whale that ends whale.

What's a horse's motto?
You get what you neigh for.

What's a cautious caterpillar's motto?
Look before you creep.

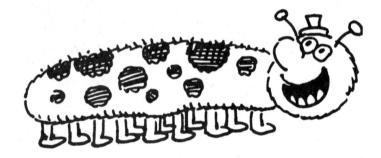

20
Childish and Wildish

Where do you learn how to take care of sick people?
In nurse-ry school.

Why do we dress baby girls in pink and baby boys in blue?
Because they can't dress themselves.

Why didn't the girl go to work in the beauty parlor?
Because she was too young to dye (die).

Who is Mr. Coffee's favorite nursery rhyme character?
Little Boy Brew.

What two-ton animal went to the ball and lost her glass slipper?

    Cinderella-phant.

What did Jack the Giant Killer name his poodle?

    Fifi Fie Fo Fum.

How did the fairy godmother get to the 95th floor?

    She took the Cinderella-vator.

What is an elephant's favorite fairy tale?

    "The Princess and the Peanut."

What superhero makes the best sandwiches?
Wonder Bread Woman.

What sheep got involved with 40 thieves?
Ali Baa Baa.

Where do gnomes pay to cross bridges?
At troll booths.

What did E.T. tell Dr. Watson?
"Phone Holmes."

What do you call a superhero with no personality?
A superzero.

What flavor of soda does the Creature from the Black Lagoon like to drink?
Lemon and slime.

What degrees did the black sheep get from college?
> *BA, BA.*

Why didn't the shepherd get a good night's sleep?
> *He walked in his sheep.*

What's a magician's favorite nursery rhyme?
> *"Trickery, Dickory, Dock."*

Why do sheep make good lawyers?
> *Because you can't pull the wool over their eyes.*

What's a baby virus' favorite song?
> *"Pop Goes the Measle."*

What's black and white, black and white, black and white and red?
> *Three skunks fighting over a stawberry.*

Why didn't Dorothy's friend the Scarecrow spend his allowance before going to Oz?
> *He was saving for a brainy day.*

Who had the greasiest gun in the Old West?
> *The Crisco Kid.*

What athletes went up the hill to fetch a pail of water?
> *Jock and Jill.*

What brand of crayon sobs at the drop of a hat?
Cry-ola.

What does a little snake have when it doesn't get its way?
Hiss-terics.

What do headhunters learn at day camp?
Darts and crafts.

What do Santa's reindeer learn in school?
Their Sleigh, B, Cs.

What do choir students do after they finish their homework?
Their hymnwork.

What rabbit team held up banks?
Bunny and Clyde.

What gangster couple bungled every bank robbery they planned?
Bonnie and Clod.

How do you greet a rich baby?
"Gucci, Gucci, coo."

How did Stephen King learn to write horror novels?
Trial and terror.

Who was the most unfriendly pilgrim?
  Miles Standoffish.

Why did the Lone Ranger hire a maid?
  To polish his High Ho Silver.

Who gets hit with a pie on Christmas?
  Ebenezer Stooge.

Where do you go to buy loud games?
  Noise R Us.

What's pink, has a curly tail and drinks blood?
  A hampire.

Why do skeletons go to college?
  They get skullerships.

What's the difference between a gorilla
and a pizza?
  If you don't know,
  remind me not to
  send you shopping.

What is the most important thing
little witches learn in school?
  How to spell.

What kind of school do little witches go to?
  Charm school.

What grizzly has been married dozens of times?
Zsa Zsa Ga-bear.

What do famous wolves become members of?
The Howl of Fame.

What's the difference between Elvis Presley, Betty Crocker, and the oldest man in the world?
One shakes, one bakes, and one aches.

What's the difference between your feet and your nose?
If your feet run you're quick, but if your nose runs you're sick.

What do you sing to a parrot when it's one year old?
"Happy Bird-day to you . . ."

What kind of music do you hear on the playground?
Swing.

Why did the bride borrow an aardvark and a freezing goat?
*So she could have something burrowed and
something blue*

Where do you find aardvarks?
That depends on where you put them.

21
Fool-Time Jobs

How do you begin a detective story?
"Once upon a crime . . ."

Where can you read about famous detectives?
In "Clue's Who."

What's the difference between a marine biologist and a happy dog?
One tags his whale, the other wags his tail.

When do barbers set their clocks ahead?
During daylight-shaving time.

When are tailors most difficult to be around?
When they're having a fit.

What does a chimney sweep wear
to work?
Soot (suit) and tie.

Who drives away all his customers?
A cab driver.

What do women gardeners wear to get married?
Weeding dresses.

What's the difference between a china shop and a furniture shop?
One sells tea-sets, the other sells settees.

What's the difference between a good football player and an efficient man?
One times his passes well, the other passes his time well.

What's the difference between a milkmaid and a seagull?
One skims milk, the other skims water.

What do undertakers carry their papers in?
Griefcases.

What's the difference between a presidential candidate and an overworked secretary?

> *One can't wait to get in office and one can't wait to get out of the office.*

What would you get if you crossed an accountant, a pickle and Miss Universe?

> *A tall, green woman who can file taxes and her nails at the same time.*

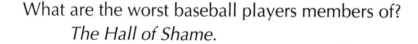

What insect plays the worst game of football?

> *The fumblebee.*

What are the worst baseball players members of?
> *The Hall of Shame.*

What's a matador's favorite sport?
> *Basketbull.*

What's the difference between a water barrel and a bad baseball player?

> *One catches the drops, the other drops the catches.*

What would you get if you crossed an acrobat with a Good Samaritan?

> *Someone who really bends over backwards to help.*

What would you get if you crossed an illustrator with an executioner?

> *An artist who draws pictures and then hangs them at dawn.*

What would you get if you crossed a parachute with a distant relative?

> *A skydiver who drops in on you at the most inconvenient time.*

What's the difference between a dressmaker and a farmer?

A dressmaker sews what she gathers, a farmer gathers what he sows.

What's the difference between a cashier and a school teacher?

One minds the till, the other tills the mind.

What's the difference between a retired sailor and a blind man?

One cannot go to sea, the other cannot see to go.

What would you get if you crossed a magician with a shopaholic?

Someone who makes money disappear.

What would you get if you crossed a police officer with a gambler?

A meter maid who gives out lottery tickets.

What banker snitches on his friends?
A tattle-teller.

Why did the actor need a calculator?
For subtraction and audition.

What does a magician say when he takes a picture?
"Focus pocus."

What would you get if you crossed a kitten, a hyena, and a millionaire?

A fat cat who laughs all the way to the bank.

What would you get if you crossed a rabbit with an amoeba?

A bunny that can multiply and divide itself.

What do boxers wear to tell time?

Fist watches.

What did Union soldiers do for fun during the American Civil War?

Yankee panky.

Why did the waiter look grumpy?

Because he had a chip on his shoulder.

What did the dentist say to the gopher?

"You have a hole in one."

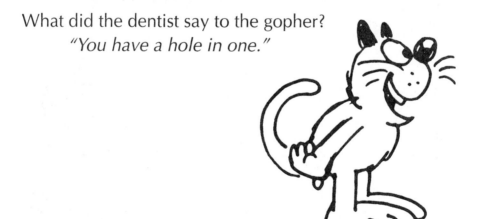

22
Oddities and Entities

What large, horned animal casts spells?
A rhinosorceress.

What do witches read to their babies to help them sleep?
Dreadtime stories.

What must you take if you want to ride Pegasus, the winged horse?
Horseback gliding lessons.

Who is the Greek and Roman god of stupidity?
Jerkules.

What beauty contest did Venus, the goddess of love, win?
Myth Universe.

What is Zeus' favorite subject?
Mythematics.

What's the first thing Zeus puts on in the morning?
His thunderware.

Where did King Midas live after he retired?
In a gold age home.

Why were the Dark Ages so dark?
They had more knights (nights) in those days.

What knight wore tap shoes?
Sir Dancelot.

What would you get if you crossed axes and twigs?
Chopsticks.

Where did James Bond live after he retired?
In an old agent home.

What superheroine always messes things up?
   Blunder Woman.

What did the nudist say to the mirror?
   "Who's the barest one of all?"

How do vampires like to travel?
   By scareplane.

How do you wake up a dragon?
   With a fire alarm.

What's a ghoul's favorite holiday song?
   "I'll Be Gnome for Christmas."

What's a troll's favorite cowboy song?
"Gnome on the Range."

Who serves ice cream faster than a speeding bullet?
Scooperman.

Who got yelled at for breaking into a house owned by three bears?
Scoldilocks.

Who is the strangest person in Emerald City?
The Wizard of Odd.

Where do spies shop?
At the snoopermarket.

Why are your nose and your handkerchief deadly enemies?
> *Because when they meet they come to blows.*

Why was the tiger made sergeant in the army?
> *Because he had the stripes.*

Which branch of the air force do parrots join?
> *The parrot-troopers.*

What's the difference between a needle and a cyclops?
> *They both have eyes, but a needle's is easier to thread.*

What's the difference between a cyclops and a needle?
> *They both have eyes, but a cyclops is easier to find in a haystack.*

Why did the cyclops read *Playboy* magazine?
> *He had an eye for the ladies.*

What do you get when you cross Toto with Godzilla?
> *A little monster that goes to Oz and swallows the Yellow Brick Road.*

What would you get if you crossed a vampire with an Avon lady?
> *I don't know, but when it rings the doorbell, don't answer it.*

Why was the Bride of Frankenstein always dieting?
She wanted to keep her ghoulish figure.

What sorceress thumbs rides on brooms?
A witchhiker.

What did Casper win for being the friendliest ghost?
A boo-by prize.

How do you begin a ghost story?
"Once upon a tomb . . ."

What do mummies wear on Halloween?
Cos-tombs.

What do mummies dance to?
Wrap music.

What would you get if you crossed Dracula with a termite?
A vampire who gets a wooden stake through his heart and then eats it.

Why did Dracula quit his job?
It was nothing that he could sink his teeth into.

What's the most frightening kind of bee?
A zom-bee.

Where do zombies live?
On dead-end streets.

Why don't zombies get invited to most celebrations?
Because they're never the life of the party.

What's a zombie's favorite party game?
Died 'n' Seek.

What's a zombie's favorite sport?
Casketball.

What boxing title did King Kong try to win?
Heavyweight chimp.

What do witches spread on their bagels?
Scream cheese.

How did Noah get ballerinas onto the ark?
Tutu by tutu.

What ghost is always welcome in December?
The Christmas spirit.

What phone company do aliens use to call home?
E. T. & T.

23
Moving Right Along

What car can't stop talking?
Chatty Chatty Bang Bang.

What do you have when a Honda Accord gets into a
head-on collision?
An Accord-ion.

What happens when an expensive German car smashes
into a light post?
The Mercedes Benz (bends).

When does poison ivy get caught in traffic?
During rash (rush) hour.

Why did the Easter Bunny get a ticket?
For running a hop sign.

What car lives in a bell tower?
The Hatchback of Notre Dame.

What is a semi's favorite sport?
Truck and field.

What's the difference between a parade float and a kitchen sink?
You can sink a float, but you can't float a sink.

What's the difference between a red carpet and a deodorant stick?
One you roll out and the other you roll on.

What would you get if you crossed Einstein with a sleepwalker?
A lazy student who gets A's while getting ZZZ's.

Why did the Mexican beans go to the psychiatrist?
They were a bit jumpy.

What would you get if you crossed a Ferrari with a belching dragon?
A car that never runs out of gas.

What would you get if you crossed an ostrich with a mobster?

A long-necked gangster who buries someone else's head in the sand.

What would you get if you crossed a Boy Scout with his grandmother?

Someone who can help himself across the street.

What would you get if you crossed Babe Ruth with a fugitive?

A baseball player who hits the ball and then runs away from home.

What did the volcano say to the other volcano?

"I lava you."

What did the ship say when asked when it wanted to sail?
"The schooner the better."

How does Moby Dick like his steak cooked?
Whale (well) done.

What do you have when two ox-drawn plows collide?
An oxident.

Which ocean won the race?
Neither, they tide.

What did German settlers drive in the Old West?
Covered Volkswagens.

Why did the chicken walk down the street?
Because it didn't have change for a bus.

What natural disaster moves too fast to be seen clearly?
A blurricane.

Do you have to be rich to ride in your own carriage?
Not if you're a baby.

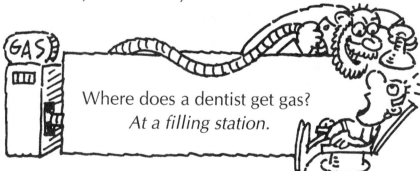

Where does a dentist get gas?
At a filling station.

Flower Power

What flowers do you send a squirrel on
Valentine's Day?
Forget-me-nuts.

What flowers do you send a ballerina?
Tutu-lips.

What flowers do you send a comedian?
Laugh-odils.

What flowers do you send a Russian king?
Czar-nations.

What flowers do you send a fish?
Pe-tunas.

What flowers do you send a snake?
Hiss-anthemums.

What flowers do you send Pinocchio?
Lie-lacs.

What does your true love give to you on the last day of Fall?
A partridge in a bare tree.

What Native American tribe does Santa belong to?
The Navaho-ho-hos.

What Native American brought down the Ten Commandments?
Geronimoses.

Why did the baby moon get punished?
For staying out all night.

Why was the mother star disappointed when she had a little daughter?
She wanted a little sun.

24
Wild and Crazy

What famous dog bakes cakes?
Betty Cocker.

What do you say when Betty Crocker comes out on the baseball field?
"Batter up!"

What is the saddest dog?
A melan-collie.

What command did the vet give the sick dog?
Heal.

Prehysterical Creatures

What prehistoric animals ate in all-night restaurants?
Diner-saurs.

What prehistoric animal did everything in a hurry?
The prontosaurus.

Where did cavemen go to buy a brontosaurus?
To a dinostore.

What does a brontosaurus do when it sleeps?
Dinosnores.

What do monkeys plant in their rock gardens?
Chimpansies.

Why wouldn't the groundhog leave his hole on February 2nd?
Because he was scared of his own shadow.

What does a schnauzer do when it sleeps?
Schnores.

What do you call a German shepherd with spots?
A German leopard.

What did Elvis teach his dog?
To rock 'n' roll over.

How did the rooster leave town?
He flew the coop.

What would you get if you crossed a chicken with peanut butter?
Eggs that stick to the roof of your mouth.

Why did the monkey go bananas?
He couldn't figure out whether he was his brother's keeper or his keeper's brother.

Where did Porky keep his money?
  In a piggy bank.

Where do Eskimos keep their hogs?
  In pigloos.

How does a shy rodent give money to charity?
  Anony-mouse-ly.

What is the stupidest animal in the deer family?
  A doe-doe.

What is the toughest kind of toad?
  A bullyfrog.

What lizard tells little white lies?
  An amfibian.

What grasshopper was born in June?
  Gemini (Jiminy) Cricket.

What do you call a rabbit's wives?
  His hare-m.

What cafeteria is owned by chickens?
  A roosterant.

What famous bear wrote scary stories?
  Edgar Allan Pooh.

What cuddly bear complains all the time?
  Whine-y-the-Pooh.

What do you get when baby bears stay out in the cold too long?
  Ice cubs.

How is a teddy bear like a person with a cold?
  They both have stuffed noses.

Horsing Around

Where do horses say "I do?"
  On the bridal path.

Why did the mother horse wake up in a sweat?
  She had a nightmare.

Where do horses commit crimes?
  In bad neigh-borhoods.

What did the horse say to the nagging jockey?
  "Get off my back."

Why can't horses tap dance?
  Their shoes are too tight.

What do you call a knight on horseback who
leaps over 16 dragons?
  Medieval Knievel.

When do Donald and Daffy Duck wake-up?
At the quack of dawn.

What do you get when Mickey and Minnie Mouse stay out in the cold too long?
Mice cubes.

How does Dumbo call his friends?
On the elephone.

What does a cat say when it stubs its toe?
"Meow-ch!"

Pony Baloney

What do you say to a pony who claims he can fly?

"Horse feathers!"

What do you call a pony who snitches on his best friend?

A tattletail.

What do you get when you hitch a pony to a small plastic bag?

A horse and baggie.

When does a talking pony stop talking?
When it's horse (hoarse).

What do you get when you cross a stray cat with a crocodile?

> *An alley gator.*

Who rents the dumbest movies?

> *A vidiot.*

Who has orange hair and a red nose and can make it rain?

> *Bozo the Cloud.*

What kind of bird goes to church on Sunday?

> *A bird of pray.*

Where do ravens hang out?

> *At the crowbar.*

How do ducks think?

> *They pond-er.*

Why are pelicans always in debt?

> *Because they have large bills.*

Why do fish have such huge phone bills?

> *Because once they get on the line they can't get off.*

25
Out and About

What did Lawrence of Arabia say after walking across the Sahara desert?

"Long time no sea."

What happens when Canada loses its balance?

Niagara Falls.

What happens when a pyramid falls into the ocean?

It sphinx (sinks).

What did one hair say to the other hair?
    "It takes two to tangle."

Where do Russians get milk?
    From Mos-cows.

What do you get when a cow stumbles?
    Chipped beef.

Which farm animal won't drink real coffee?
    De calf.

What young farm animal was an outlaw in the Wild West?
    Billy Goat the Kid.

What is an astrologer's favorite vegetable?
Capri-corn on the cob.

What vegetable is green, gooey, and grows in the Black Lagoon?
Slime-a beans.

How does Mr. Fixit put vegetables back together?
With tomato paste.

Where do weeds stand and wait?
In dandelines.

How can you tell if a potato is asleep?
See if its eyes are closed.

What do you get when you cross a daytime drama with a talk show?

A soap Oprah.

What do hamburgers exchange when they get married?

Onion rings.

What do roosters take with them on every trip?

Their combs.

What would you get if you crossed a hen with a bear?

A chicken that sleeps all winter.

What does Benji eat at the movies?

Pupcorn.

Out to Lunch

What does Superman eat for lunch?
A hero sandwich.

What does a computer operator eat for lunch?
Floppy joes.

What does a sloppy joe become when it rains?
A soppy joe.

What does a mail carrier eat for lunch?
A bacon, letters and tomato sandwich.

What dessert is easy to make?
A piece of cake.

What is Minnie Mouse's favorite dessert?
Cheesecake.

What did the body builder eat at the Mexican restaurant?
   Machos.

What is Bullwinkle's favorite flavor of ice cream?
   Chocolate moose.

What is a miser's favorite flavor of ice cream?
   Chocolate cheap.

What's a shark's favorite ice cream?
   Fin-illa.

What did the leopard say after he finished his dinner?
   "That hit the spot."

What would you get if you crossed an eel with a goat?
An electric can opener.

Why didn't anyone get angry with the baby goat when it played a practical joke?
It was just kid-ding around.

How do you let the Munsters know you're at their front door?
Ring the buzzard.

Why did they pour rubbing alcohol into the ocean?
They had some sore mussels.

Where did the priest spend his time when he was a baby?
In a pray pen.

How do you know a clock is hungry?
It goes back for seconds.

How many sides does every building have?
Two—the inside and the outside.

What's the hardest glass to wash?
Stained glass.

What do a snakes's towels say?
"Hiss" and "Hers."

Why did the old house see the doctor?
It was having window panes.

Where do coins go to bed at night?
In sleeping quarters.

When does a dimwit go to bed?
When he's nincom-pooped.

What has six feet and can't move?
Two yards.

How did the man tiling the bathroom wall explain the mistakes?
Tile and error.

Where do wealthy plants grow?
In jackpots.

What do a gladiator's towels say?
"Ben-His" and "Ben-Hurs."

What should you do when a mouse squeaks?
Oil it.

26
Nobody's Business

How does a bullfighter enter the ring?
> *Through the mata-door.*

What is the first thing a prizefighter does when he gets to work?
> *Punches the time clock.*

What kind of bread likes to make speeches?
> *Toast.*

What's the most popular game in the bank?
Show 'n' Teller.

What do orthodontists do when they like you?
Try to make a good impression.

What do you get when lightning strikes Wall Street?
A shock market.

How does a cowboy make decisions?
On the spur of the moment.

Why did the baker fire the bread?
He caught it loafing.

What do federal investigators do when they go to sleep at night?
They close their F. B. eyes.

How do police officers transport hamburgers to jail?
In patty wagons.

When you kill someone with kindness, what do you get charged with?
Assault and flattery.

What do you get when you cross a detective and a crocodile?

A private investi-gator.

Why was the angry man so stupid?

Because he gave everyone a piece of his mind.

What do mail carriers do when they're angry?

Stamp their feet.

When did the army break down?

When it was out of orders.

Why shouldn't you play with matches?

Because you could make an ash of yourself.

Why was the electrician arrested?
For assault and battery.

How does the owner of a hot dog stand wear her hair?
In a bun.

When do cowboys get married?
When they want to saddle down.

Why couldn't the handsome baseball player get married?
He wanted to play the field.

What happened when the soldier got lost at the art sale?
He was reported missing in auction.

Where do cowboys get their hair cut?
In beauty saloons.

Why did the Japanese chef yell?
He lost his tempura.

Why did the artist yell?
He lost his tempera.

What did the French chef give his girlfriend when he escorted her home?
A quiche (kiss) goodnight.

What did the jack say to the car?
"Can I give you a lift?"

27
Creepy Crawly

Why was the bee dancing on top of the honey jar?
The sign said, "Twist to open."

What does the little bee want to be when he grows up?
A buzz driver.

What does a bee wear while exercising?
A swarm-up suit.

What's smarter than a talking parrot?
A spelling bee.

Why do bumblebees hum?
They forgot the words.

Why do you call an exterminator to work on your computer?
To get the bugs out.

How did the insect avoid jail?
By flea bargaining.

How do wasps catch drug dealers?
In sting operations.

What happened when the two boa constrictors met?
They got a crush on each other.

Why do you carry a snake on the front of your car?
That's our windshield viper.

Where do rich snakes keep their hired help?
In the serpent's quarters.

What kind of snake eats airplanes?
A Boeing constrictor.

Why didn't the two snakes on the Ark go forth and multiply as Noah suggested?
They were both adders.

When does a poisonous snake bite?
When it's hissed off.

What are we going to do with that 100-pound worm in the garden?
Find a 1,000-pound pigeon.

What worms like music?
Tape worms.

What do worms do in the cornfield?
They go in one ear and out the other.

What's brown and long and seldom rings?
An unlisted earthworm.

How can you tell which end of the worm is its head?
Tickle the middle with a feather and see which end sneezes.

Why can't you milk a worm?
Because there's no stool low enough to fit under it.

What animals came into the Ark in pairs?
I don't know, but worms came in apples.

What would you get if you crossed a boa constrictor with an orange?

An animal that squeezes its own juice.

Why did the snake collect a pension from the government?

He was a civil serpent.

Why was the rattlesnake feeling sick?

He bit his lip.

What do you call a Roman boa constrictor?

Julius Squeezer.

What snake makes a good policeman?

A copperhead.

Why does it take so long to cross a pit viper with a pit bull?
It's hard to get rid of all those pits.

Can moths swim?
Yes, they do the butterfly.

Who was the original skin diver?
The mosquito.

Where do people sit around and watch insects?
At cricket matches.

Which insects sleep with sheets and pillow cases?
Bedbugs.

What do you get when you cross a praying mantis and a termite?
An insect that says grace before devouring your house.

28
Party Animals

What Australian animal loves to dance?
The tangoroo.

What do astronauts dance to?
Rocket 'n' roll music.

What do dancers climb?
Fred Astairs.

What's a tornado's favorite dance?
The twist.

What do dragons serve with cheese at parties?
>   *Firecrackers.*

What does a polar bear like on his birthday cake?
>   *Icing.*

What's the difference between a Jack-in-the-Box and a party crasher?
>   *One pops out when the music stops, and one pops in when the music starts.*

What do gamblers serve at birthday parties?
>   *Cake and dice cream.*

Who helped the cow go to the ball?
Its dairy godmother.

What did Mickey Mouse say to his girlfriend on her birthday?
"Minnie happy returns."

Did the stick of dynamite enjoy the party?
Yes, it had a blast.

Why do flies carry stopwatches at parties?
Because flies time when they're having fun.

What did Cinderella's pet seal wear to the ball?
A glass flipper.

What did one tropical bird say to the other tropical bird?
"Toucan play at that game."

What's a vampire's favorite game?
Follow the bleeder.

What's a bee's favorite game?
Hive 'n' seek.

What's a baby thief's favorite game?
Sneak-a-boo.

What does Mr. Spock perform at parties?
Magic treks.

What is Dr. Jekyll's favorite game?
Hyde 'n' Seek.

How do you keep a gorilla from crashing your party?
Send him an invitation.

What's a lazy toad's favorite game?
Sleep frog.

29
Everybody Eats!

What did the hippie feed his dogs?
Groovy Train.

What does Pinocchio feed his wooden dog?
Puppet Chow.

What does a witch serve her friends?
A full-curse meal.

What do camels eat in the desert?
Sandwiches.

How do you make a hot dog stand?
Steal its chair.

What's Santa's favorite sandwich?
Peanut butter and jolly.

What do kittens drink?
Condensed milk.

What candy do award-winning television stars eat?
M & Emmys.

What sound does a barber's cereal make?
"Snip, crackle, pop."

What sound does a chicken's cereal make?
"Snap, crackle, peep."

What do cats put on frankfurters?
  Moustard.

What's a cat's favorite dessert?
  Mice cream.

What's the difference between a turkey and a house guest?
  One is stuffed before dinner and one is stuffed after dinner.

What's the difference between a peanut and a turtle?
  Both have shells, but a peanut is easier to eat.

What's the difference between an orchestra conductor and an oven?
  One makes the beat, the other bakes the meat.

How do vegetables win a race?
  They cross the spinach (finish) line.

What's an Eskimo's favorite vegetable?
  Mushed potatos.

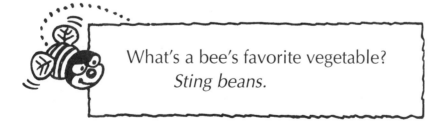

What's a bee's favorite vegetable?
  Sting beans.

What happens when an onion tells a joke?
You laugh and cry at the same time.

What do pizza makers put on their eggs?
Salt and pepper-oni.

Where do you bring a salad that's not yours?
To the Tossed and Found.

What's the messiest vegetable?
Corn on the slob.

What does a slob's Jack-in-the-Box play?
"Slop Goes the Weasel."

What's the scariest vegetable?
Corn on the Blob.

What do tarantulas eat?
Burgers and flies.

What's a frog's favorite snack?
Croaker Jacks.

What is Kareem Abdul Jabbar's favorite dessert?
Ice Kareem.

What do you get when someone spills ice cream on James Bond?
Spy à la mode.

Where do criminals find the recipe for a cake that has a file in it?
In a crookbook.

When is a Chinese restaurant successful?
When it makes a fortune, cookie.

What is the difference between a zoo and a delicatessen?
A zoo has a man-eating tiger, and a delicatessen has a man eating salami.

What is the difference between a sharpshooter and a delicious meal?
One hits the mark, the other hits the spot.

What is the difference between the sun and a loaf of bread?
One rises from the east, the other from the yeast.

30
Go Fish!

Why was the catfish covered with bandages?
He got into a dogfight.

How did the fish's hearing improve?
He got a new herring aid.

What would you get if you crossed a 747 and a flounder?
A flying fish.

What is your fish's favorite game show on TV?
"Eel of Fortune."

How do we know fish are concerned about their weight?
They carry their scales everywhere.

Why are fish so fond of salt water?
Because pepper makes them sneeze.

Why did they let a fish in the operating room?
He was a sturgeon (surgeon).

Where do fish sleep?
In waterbeds.

How do you keep a fish from smelling?
Clamp a clothespin over its nose.

Why did they disband the all-fish, country-and-western band?

> *They couldn't find a bass player.*

Where did they take the whale to get it weighed?

> *To the whale-weigh station.*

What's a shark's favorite food?

> *Submarine sandwiches.*

What's worse than seeing a shark's eye while you're swimming?

> *Staring at his tonsils.*

Where do shellfish sue for damages?

> *In small clams court.*

Does an octopus make a good pet?

> *Are you squidding?*

What would you get if you crossed an eagle with a salmon?

> *An animal that flies upstream to spawn.*

31
Time Off

What would you get if you crossed a steer with a porcupine?

A steak with a built-in toothpick.

Why did the porcupine buy so many ballpoint pens?

He was tired of using quills.

Do porcupines get much mail?

No, they only have two litters (letters) a year

What's yellow, very dangerous and flies?
A canary with a machine gun.

What would you get if you crossed a canary with a 30-foot snake?
A sing-a-long.

What would you get if you crossed a bird with a piece of furniture?
A stool pigeon.

What keys don't open doors?
Turkeys, monkeys and donkeys.

Why did the duck have catsup all over his face?
He told the waitress to put it on his bill.

Which is correct—Bill or William?
Have you ever seen a duck eat corn with its William?

Why did the girl take her rabbit to the barber shop?
It needed a hare cut.

What boat has no class?
A riff raft.

211

What should you groom a rabbit with?
Hare spray.

Where do rabbits go after the wedding?
On a bunnymoon.

What hen never goes out on the slopes at a winter resort?
Chicken of the ski.

How could you tell the bird liked his home?
He wouldn't stop raven about it.

What does Scoobby Doo like to do on vacation?
Scoobby dive.

What would you get if you crossed a pig, a sheep and a fir tree?

A pork-ewe-pine.

How do you save a drowning rodent?

Give him mouse-to-mouse resuscitation.

What did the big boat say to the little boat?

"You're a ship off the old dock."

Why was the beach a winner?

Because it was shore of itself.

What is the funniest motorcycle?

A Yamahaha.

Why did the seal cross the road?

To get to the otter side.

What ape can jump higher than a coconut tree?

Most of them. Coconut trees can't jump.

Where do you send a turtle to buy gas?

To the Shell station.

How do turtles keep warm?

They wear people-neck sweaters.

Where did Hiawatha drive his sports car?
On the hia-way.

What do you put on a young locomotive to teach it how to run?
Training wheels.

What would Santa be if he quit working and stole rides on freight trains?
A ho-ho-hobo.

Are elephants allowed on 747s?
Only if they check their trunks.

What is black and white and yellow, goes up and down, but never touches the ground?

A zebra and a canary riding in an elevator.

What's black and white, black and white, black and white . . . ?

A zebra rolling downhill.

What's black and white and red all over?

A zebra with the measles.

Where do swimmers sit to eat lunch?

At pool tables.

How do you take pictures of a swimming pool?

With splash cubes.

What birds are always sad?
Blue jays.

What is the soft, mushy stuff between a shark's teeth?
Slow swimmers.

What do squirrels give each other on Valentine's day?
Forget-me-nuts.

What would you get if you crossed an absent-minded professor with an insect?
A forget-me-gnat.

Did you hear about the girl who was engaged to a fellow with a wooden leg?
Her father broke it off.

32
Baseball
and Other Games

What serious traffic violation is allowed in baseball?
Hit-and-run.

Why did the baseball batter take his car to the game?
It's a long drive to center field.

Who lives under a tree and hits home runs?
Babe Root.

What did they call the dog that belonged to the baseball player?

The catcher's mutt.

How can you pitch a winning baseball game without throwing a ball?

Throw only strikes.

What's the difference between a soft ball and a hard ball?

The difference between a lump on the head and a brain concussion.

What is a personal foul?

A chicken of your own.

Why do fast-food lovers make good joggers?
Because they like to eat and run.

Where should a jogger wash his sneakers?
In running water.

What happened when the jogger slammed into a pile of IOU's?
He ran into debt.

What flavor jam do cheerleaders like best?
Rahs-berry.

What smells nice and rides a horse?
The Cologne Ranger.

What did the bowling ball say to the bowling pin?
"I'll spare you this time."

Why do soccer players get good grades in school?
They use their heads.

What do baseball players on third base sing?
"There's No Place Like Home."

What's the difference between a rain gutter and a bad fielder?
One catches drops, the other drops catches.

Who lives in a pod and knows Kung Fu?
Bruce Pea.

What tree knows Kung Fu?
Spruce Lee.

Where do gorillas exercise?
On jungle gyms.

33
Don't You Dare!

What do you call a monster who devours everything in its path?

> *Lonesome.*

When did Dr. Frankenstein stop being lonely?

> *When he learned how to make new friends.*

Why did the Frankenstein monster go out with a prune?

> *Because he couldn't get a date.*

Who do sea monsters date?

> *They go out with the tide.*

Who do ghouls date?
Anyone they can dig up.

What did the stamp say to the envelope?
"I'm stuck on you."

Where do ghosts pick up their mail?
At the ghost office.

How does a letter from a ghost begin?
"Tomb (to whom) it may concern . . ."

What does a ghost bride throw to her bridesmaids?
A boo-quet (bouquet).

How do you kiss a hockey player?
You pucker up.

Why are crows so noisy when they use the phone?
They're making long distance caws.

How do vampires kiss?
Very carefully..

What did the boy monster say to the girl monster?
"I want to hold your hand, hand, hand, hand . . ."

What song do monsters sing about their girlfriends?
"The Ghoul That I Marry . . ."

Why did the boy monster whistle at the girl monster?
Because she had nice legs, legs, legs, legs . . .

What vegetable do you get when a monster steps on a house?
Mushed rooms.

What monster is crazy about locks?
The Lock Nuts monster.

How To Be Really Popular

Why are gravediggers popular?
Because they're so down-to-earth.

Why are undertakers so popular?
Because they're the last ones to let you down.

Why are mad doctors so popular?
Because they're such cut-ups.

Why are Abominable Snowmen so popular?
Because they're so cool.

Why are vampires popular?
Because they get under your skin.

Why are giants popular?
Because people look up to them.

How To Be Really Unpopular

Why don't people like vampires?
Because they're a pain in the neck.

Why don't people like executioners?
Because they're always hanging around.

Why don't people like Abominable Snowmen?
Because it's too hard to warm up to them.

Why don't people like mummies?
Because they're all wrapped up in themselves.

Why don't people like skeletons?
Because they've got no heart.

What's the best thing to do if you find a gorilla in your bed?
Sleep somewhere else.

That Monster Is So Repulsive—

—How Repulsive Is He?

He's so repulsive that when he throws a boomerang it doesn't come back.

He's so repulsive that when he plays hide-and-seek nobody looks for him.

He's so repulsive that when he goes to the zoo, the monkeys throw peanuts at him.

Where do fortune-tellers dance?
   At the crystal ball.

Where do Abominable Snowmen dance?
   At the snowball.

Why didn't the skeleton go to the dance?
   He had nobody (no body) to go with.

What music do mummies dance to?
Ragtime.

What is seven feet high, green and sits in the corner?
The Incredible Sulk.

What do elves sing when they are depressed?
"Gnome, gnome on the range . . ."

What seafood does Godzilla like?
Submarine sandwiches.

When Godzilla goes out for dinner, what does he eat?
The restaurant.

Why did Godzilla eat Tokyo instead of Rome?
Because he wasn't in the mood for Italian food.

What monster has the worst luck?
The Luck Less Monster.

What did the girl Frankenstein monster say to the boy Frankenstein monster?
"You're so electrocute."

Did Count Dracula ever get married?
No, he was a bat-chelor (bachelor).

Why is Godzilla a big hit at parties?
Because he is tons of fun.

Why are werewolves a big hit at parties?
Because they're a howl.

Why don't zombies get more invitations?
Because they're never the life of the party.

What do vampires sing when the party is over?
"Auld Fang Syne."

What happened when the werewolf met the starlet?
It was love at first bite.

What did the boy rattlesnake say to the girl rattlesnake?
"Give me a little hiss."

34

You've Got
To Be Joking

What would you get if a dinosaur stepped on your foot?
   Anklosaurus.

What would you get if a prehistoric animal swallowed a lemon?
   A dino-sour.

What would you get if two prehistoric monsters crashed into each other at 60 m.p.h.?

Tyrannosaurus wrecks (rex).

What would you get if you crossed a prehistoric monster and a witch?

A Tyrannosaurus hex.

What would you get if you crossed a supermarket with big jungle animals?

Long lions at the checkout.

Why is a prune a better fighter than a hen?

Because the prune isn't chicken.

What do you call a chicken who's afraid of nothing?
"Dinner."

What happened to the kitten who fell in love with the Xerox machine?
It became a copycat.

Where do carpenters study?
Boarding school.

What is a carpenter's favorite dessert?
Pound cake.

What is St. Peter's favorite dessert?
Angel cake.

What's a tree's favorite drink?
Root beer.

What does a polite electrician say when you do him a favor?

"Thanks a watt!"

What is a miner's favorite game?

Mine-opoly.

What is an astronaut's favorite game?

Moon-opoly.

How do astronauts bring their food to work?

In launch boxes.

What did the computer say when it saw the computer programmers having a little snack?

"Give me a byte!"

What did the computer programmers have for a little snack?
Microchips.

What do you get when you cross a computer programmer and an Olympic athlete?
A floppy discus thrower.

What happened to the plastic surgeon when he got too close to the fire?
He melted.

How is a firecracker like a jeweler?
They both make the ear ring.

What's the difference between a butcher and a night owl?
One weighs a steak, the other stays awake.

Who gets congratulated when they're down and out?
Astronauts.

What do they call cashiers in Shanghai?
Chinese checkers.

Why didn't the barber shave the man with blue eyes?
It was easier with a razor.

What jackets do firemen prefer?
Blazers.

What do monkeys wave on Flag Day?
Star-spangled bananas.

What do owls celebrate every October?
Owl-oween.

What song did they play at the Easter Bunny's wedding?
"Hare Comes the Bride."

What do they add to food in Saudia Arabia?
Sultan pepper.

Who saw the lumberman cut down the tree?
The chain saw.

Christmas

Why is the little "R" like Christmas?
It comes at the end of December.

How does Santa Claus play poker?
With Christmas cards.

Where do Santa Claus and his family stay when they are away from the North Pole?
In a ho-ho-hotel.

Who is Santa Claus's wife?
Mary Christmas.

What did Adam say the day before Christmas?
"It's Christmas, Eve."

What do cross mice send each other at Christmas?
Cross-mouse cards.

What do you give someone who has everything?
Penicillin.

Where do sheep go for sun and fun?
  To the Baa-hamas.

What do you call a hen that gets sunburned in Florida?
  Southern fried chicken.

How do baby chickens dance?
  Chick-to-chick.

How do Arabians dance?
  Sheik-to-sheik.

How do ghosts dance?
  Shriek-to-shriek.

Have you ever seen a barn dance?
  No, but I've seen a chimney sweep.

What do you get if you cross a stick of dynamite and the white of an egg?

A boom-meringue.

What do you get if you cross an alligator and a parrot?

An animal that bites your head off if you don't give it a cracker.

What do cats read each day?

Mewspapers.

What kind of cat helps you fix things?

A tool kit.

What cat was a famous Chinese leader?

Miaow Tse-tung.

What do cows like to listen to on the radio?
Moo-sic.

What kind of music do you hear at the paper cup factory?
Dixieland.

What kind of music do you hear at the Grand Canyon?
Rock.

What do you call six stones with electric guitars?
A rock group.

What happened when the king's men played a joke on Humpty-Dumpty?
He fell for it.

35
Setting Records

Who was the most brilliant animal in the world?
  Ein-swine.

Which letters are the smartest?
  The Y's (wise).

Who are the slowest talkers in the world?
  Convicts—they can spend 25 years on a single sentence.

What is the saddest piece of clothing?
  Blue jeans.

What is the saddest picture?
  A blueprint.

What door is the saddest?
  A revolving door, because everyone is always pushing it around.

What is the oldest fruit?
　　Adam's apple.

Who was the straightest man in the Bible?
　　Joseph, because Pharaoh made him a ruler.

Did you hear about the highest paid acrobat in the world?
　　He flies through the air with the greatest of fees.

Who is the best contortionist in the world?
The sailor who sits on his chest.

Which is the smartest pickle?
The one that uses its brine (brain).

What beam weighs the least?
A moon beam.

What is the best-looking geometric figure?
Acute angle.

36
This Is The End!

Why do demons and ghouls get along so well?
>   *Because demons are a ghoul's best friends.*

What four letters do you ask a friend who just met Dracula?
>   *R-U-O-K.*

What four letters would really surprise the Invisible Man?
>   *O-I-C-U.*

What is the first thing a witch rings for in a hotel?
>   *B-room service.*

Why do witches fly brooms?
>   *Because vacuum cleaners don't have long enough cords.*

What is green and wrinkled and goes through walls?
    Casper, the Friendly Pickle.

What would you hear if you crossed a witch's broom and a clock?
    The broom's tick (broomstick).

What is yellow, makes webs and jumps from building to building?
    Spider Banana.

What wears a black cape, flies through the air and bites people?
    A mosquito in a black cape.

Did you hear about the monster who went to the beauty parlor?
> *They wouldn't let her in.*

What song do monsters play at beauty pageants?
> *"A Pretty Ghoul Is Like a Malady."*

What is the most important safety rule for witches?
> *Don't fly off the handle.*

If Dracula and King Kong jumped off the top of the Empire State Building, who would land first?
> *Who cares!*

What is the difference between Count Dracula and a grape?
> *The grape is purple.*

What does Dracula visit when he goes to New York?
> *The Vampire State Building.*

What do vampires learn in business school?
> *How to type blood.*

Why did King Kong climb the Empire State Building?
> *To catch a plane.*

What did the monster eat after the dentist pulled its tooth?
> *The dentist.*

How does a graveyard love story begin?
Boy meets ghoul.

What goes around a cemetery but doesn't move?
A fence.

What do you say when you hear
a noise in the cemetery?
"Halt, who ghost there?"

How wide is a cemetery?
A grave yard.

Why was the cemetery crowded?
Everyone was dying to get in.

How far can you walk into a cemetery?
Only halfway. After that you're walking out.

Why was the ghost on the magazine cover?
Because she was BOO-tiful.

Who gives a speech after a ghost banquet?
The after-dinner spooker.

Who is the main ghost in Congress?
The Spooker (Speaker) of the House.

How do ghosts like their eggs?
Terri-fried.

If a werewolf lost its tail, where could it buy a new one?
In a retail store.

Why wouldn't Count Dracula settle down?
Because he was a fly-by-night.

Why did Count Dracula go to the orthodontist?
To improve his byte (bite).

Why was Count Dracula hanging around the computers?
He was trying to get a byte.

What happened when the dragon breathed on the computers?
He got baked Apples.

Monster Royalty Quiz

What Egyptian queen was a vampire?
Cleo-bat-ra.

Who was the biggest monarch in history?
King Kong.

What ghost haunted a King of England?
The Spirit of '76.

Why don't many ghosts go to college?
Because so few graduate from high school.

What do you say when King Kong graduates?
"Kong-gratulations!"

What do you say when Count Dracula graduates?
"Con-dracula-tions!"

What coffee does Count Dracula drink?
De-coffin-ated.

What is the most popular phone company in space?
E. T. and T.

What magazines do poltergeists read?
Good Housecreeping.

What kind of cars do ghosts drive?
Boo-icks.

What would you get if you stacked thousands of pizza pies on top of each other?
A leaning tower of pizza.

What is green and spicy and changes into a monster?
Dr. Pickle and Mr. Hyde.

Did you hear the joke about your shirt collar?
Never mind. I don't like dirty stories.

Did you hear the joke about your muscles?
Never mind. It's a lot of mush.

Did you hear the joke about your personality?
Never mind. It hasn't developed yet.

Did you hear the joke about the dropped egg?
Never mind. It cracks me up.

What did the standup comic say
when he dropped the egg on his foot?
"The yolks on me!"

When is a mummy not a mummy?
When it's a daddy.

What did one mummy say to the other
when they left each other?
"B.C.-ing you!"

Index